Steam in Cornwall

Peter W. Gray

First published 1993

ISBN 0 7110 2151 1

Published by Ian Allan Ltd, Shepperton, Surrey; and printed by Ian Allan Printing Ltd at its works at Coombelands in Runnymede, England.

Front Cover:
Five miles into the climb from Bodmin Road to Doublebois, Penzance-based 4-6-0s Nos 6808 *Beenham Grange* and 4095 *Harlech Castle* pass the derelict Cornwall Railway Westwood signalbox with the Saturdays only 9.20am from St Ives to Paddington on 13 September 1958. This long-abandoned box was built to serve the quarry used to supply stone for ballast and for rebuilding the Brunel timber viaducts in the Glynn Valley during the 1870s and 1880s. *Trevor B. Owen*

Right:
Standing at noon outside Moorswater shed, on the Liskeard-Looe branch, 2-6-2T No 5573 awaits the call of duty on Saturday 2 September 1961. Moorswater was a sub-shed of St Blazey but, on this day, with the end of steam working imminent, the branch was being worked by two strangers. No 5573 from Newton Abbot (83A) MPD was the spare engine, with scheduled early morning and often additional unscheduled afternoon workings as well, while No 4574, that month being transferred from Truro (83F) MPD to 83A, was working the timetabled passenger service. *All uncredited photographs were taken by the author*

Introduction

Welcome to Cornwall — The Royal Duchy — characterised by the Great Western Railway as the 'Cornish Riviera'.

I should like you to accompany me on a tour of the county's railways as I saw them during the closing years of the steam era. The pictures used are mostly my own, taken during the period from 1957 to 1964, but I have enlisted three friends to help me out, either with views or events that I missed. Their pictures are individually acknowledged and I should like to thank Trevor Owen, Dick Riley and Michael Mensing for allowing me to use their precious slides in this volume.

Being a Devonian, it is a privilege to be asked to prepare a book on Cornwall — my second favourite county — and one which I have visited many times, especially during those last six years to 1962 — years which saw the almost complete elimination of steam power from the old Great Western Railway system in Cornwall.

The postwar years had seen a gradual expansion of rail services into and out of Cornwall, especially on summer Saturdays. Holidays with pay, not available to many until just before the war, were now available to most of the working population and, before the era of mass car ownership, most people travelled by train when going on holiday.

Sadly, this was all to change, and far more quickly than most of us imagined possible. However, during those six years, with another two for the Southern Railway lines, I used up much of my spare time recording the railway scene here in the southwest, in black and white and in colour, not with posterity in mind, but merely so that I should have a record of what it had been like, when the steam engines had all gone. I doubt if any of us had any idea just how much the whole infrastructure of the railway would change during the next 30 years, so viewing these pictures now, against today's scene, rarely produces anything but sadness at what we have lost.

Having said that, we should be thankful that more than half the ex-GWR branch lines in Cornwall have survived in one form or another, which is more than can be said for Devon, a county that has lost most of its branches. Unfortunately, the same cannot be said for the ex-SR lines in Cornwall, which have been totally eliminated, except for the short stretch relaid by the narrow gauge Launceston Steam Railway.

If you are in, or coming to Cornwall, it goes without saying that all the remaining railways are worth a visit but, scenically, the St Ives and Gunnislake branches are, in my opinion, the most rewarding. But, although there has not been space for any pictures of them here, spare some time to seek out the visible evidence of the extinct industrial railways, which were only industrial to the extent that they were built to serve the mining industry. It can take a few days to explore thoroughly the whole length of the Liskeard & Caradon Railway and its Kilmar Tramway extension, a mineral line which served the mines in the shadow of Caradon Hill, before climbing to Minions and Cheesewring and other quarries on the scenic edge of Bodmin Moor.

In West Cornwall parts of the Poldice Tramway are being cleared to make a footpath, and there is much to see along the route of the old Redruth & Chasewater Railway.

In the north the Camel Trail follows the route of the Bodmin & Wadebridge Railway, including the LSWR extension to Padstow, and close by there is the Bodmin & Wenford Railway operating steam and diesel trains over the Bodmin General-Bodmin Road — now Parkway — line.

For those interested in the photographic details, the majority of my pictures were taken using an Agfa Super Silette 35mm camera with a magnificent fixed f2 Solagon lens, not easy to obtain in those days of import restrictions, and I should like to thank Dick Riley for suggesting the purchase of this camera, when I met him at Dainton in the summer of 1958. At that time I was using a Voigtlander Vito IIa, with a f3.5 Color-Skopar lens, which had a top shutter speed of 1/300th second, which was too fast to expose properly the Kodachrome film of that time, even in full sun. The majority of the pictures included here were taken on Kodachrome film, which had a speed of just 8ASA until the arrival, in late 1961, of Kodachrome II with a speed of 25ASA. Consequently, most of the moving trains were exposed using apertures of between f2 and f2.8 with a 1/250th second shutter speed. Today few people use films as slow as 25ASA from choice, let alone anything slower. The alternative at that time was to use Agfa CT18 — or other similar films — which, although faster, were much more grainy and often suffered from erratic processing. The experts will probably recognise a few CT18s in this selection.

Inevitably, the selection process has been difficult and alas some slides which are quite acceptable on the screen will not stand up to reproduction on the printed page; nevertheless, I think the illustrations included here give a representative view of what could have been seen during those final years. They are arranged in an order which will be familiar to those who have seen my slide shows. Starting from Saltash, we travel westwards to Penzance, including, on the way, the Southern Railway lines and all the branches south of the main line, returning from Penzance via St Ives and Newquay to conclude back at Saltash.

Finally, if any reader wishes to learn more about the 'GWR in Cornwall', he or she can do no better than to purchase the trio of books under this title by Alan Bennett, which I will admit to having consulted when preparing the captions to some of these pictures.

Peter W. Gray
Torquay
May 1993

Below:
From the fields above Coombe-by-Saltash viaduct on 25 July 1959, the second part of the summer Saturday 'Cornish Riviera Express' can be seen crossing the Royal Albert bridge into Cornwall. The train, headed by 4-6-0s Nos 7816 *Frilsham Manor* and 1021 *County of Montgomery*, is observing the 15mph speed restriction over the bridge. This train left Paddington at 10.35am, carrying portions for Penzance and Falmouth, and, after leaving Plymouth, was booked to stop at Truro, Gwinear Road and Penzance only.

The steam chain ferry, which then maintained the road link with a half-hourly service between Saltash and St Budeaux, is in mid-passage across the River Tamar. After over 700 years, this service closed in October 1961 with the opening of the new road bridge.

I.K.BRUNEL
ENGINEER
1859

Left:
Among Isambard Kingdom Brunel's finest achievements was the crossing of the River Tamar at Saltash for the Cornwall Railway. It was indeed fortunate that the Parliament of 1845 turned down the Cornwall Railway's original proposal to cross the Tamar by steam train ferry at Torpoint, causing it to turn to Mr Brunel for the survey of an alternative route.

At the time of its construction this was the greatest bridge thus far attempted and Brunel devised a unique solution, which was a development of his design for the crossing of the River Wye at Chepstow for the Great Western Railway. Each of the main spans is 455ft in length, and 100ft above high water, with seven approach spans on the Devon side and 10 on the Cornish side, leading into Saltash.

The main spans were constructed on site, on the Devon side, then floated out onto the river and gradually raised by jacks to the required height while the supporting piers were being built.

The Royal Albert Bridge celebrated its centenary on 2 May 1959 and, for that summer only, the ladders and platforms, which give access to the interior of the tubes but normally partially obscure the lettering on the end towers, were removed. Consequently, as an unidentified large prairie tank emerges into the sun with a down goods train, on Sunday 16 August 1959, we have a clear view (that may never be repeated) of the whole bridge.

On the Devon shore preparations are being made for the new road bridge and the ground is being cleared for the approach road behind the embankment and bridge carrying the Southern Region main line into Devonport and Plymouth. *Trevor B. Owen*

Above:
Leaving Saltash the main line circles the hill behind the town giving passengers a fine view across the Hamoaze towards Devonport Dockyard, before turning westwards and following the River Lynher. The original Cornwall Railway single line ran much more closely to the river bank than does the present line, which was rebuilt on a new alignment through to St Germans when the line was doubled by the GWR in 1908. The first viaduct on the 1908 line is Forder viaduct, which is being crossed by one of the 'sandwich-auto' workings, powered by 0-6-0PT No 6419 on 18 April 1960. Most of these auto workings terminated at Saltash, but this one was an except-Saturdays through working, at 12.5pm, from Plymouth to Menheniot. On Saturdays, during the winter timetable, this train left at 10.20am and proceeded through to Doublebois, returning thence at 12.30pm, to arrive back at Plymouth in good time for football or shopping.

Above:
A ganger's eye view of the Looe branch, as it climbs circuitously from the floor of the Looe River Valley, turning to the left for most of the way, but here deviating to the right as it crosses a side valley and continues the ascent under the main line. After clinging to the hillside for a while, the line then circles left again, on the outskirts of Liskeard and, climbing all the while, eventually attains the height of the main line. The main line is approached at right angles from the opposite direction, not 100yd from the end of Liskeard viaduct, and crossing it, with a clear road through the station, is an unidentified 'Grange' class 4-6-0 with a down empty vans train at 5.5pm on Sunday 6 August 1961.

Right:
With several coaches still on Liskeard viaduct, 4-6-0 No 6860 *Aberporth Grange* races in past the overlapping ends of the Liskeard station platforms with the summer Saturday 11.40am from Paddington to Penzance. This engine had only recently been transferred to Laira MPD, as the clean 83D shedplate indicates. The passengers can be assured of an exhilarating run down to Penzance, if this approach is anything to go by. The train is about 20min late and, so with some 12 stops to go, there is scope for an on time arrival at its destination.

Although the signalbox at Liskeard is still in use, together with a few semaphore signals, the water tower and telegraph poles are long since gone. Also gone is the author's Velocette LE motor cycle, without which most of these pictures would not have been taken. This can be seen parked outside the Looe line station, the roof of which is on the extreme left of the picture.

PASSENGERS ARE
REQUESTED TO CROSS
THE LINE BY MEANS
OF THE BRIDGE
9
6860
PASSENGERS ARE
REQUESTED TO CROSS
THE LINE BY MEANS
OF THE BRIDGE

LADIES
GENTLEMEN
4585

Left:
Onto the single platform of the separate Liskeard-Looe line station at Liskeard, passengers with their luggage are disembarking from the 1.11pm arrival on 29 September 1959. This branch train provided a good connection with the up 'Royal Duchy', 11.00am Penzance to Paddington service, which was due to leave Liskeard at 1.17pm.

In the background the local coal merchant appears to be sorting out his sacks, while unseen in the goods yard beyond, another 2-6-2T No 5557, is shunting. The shunter had another 12 months to go, but for No 4585 the end was near. It was withdrawn in October 1959.

Above:
As I stand with my feet in the Looe River, 2-6-2T No 4569 pulls away smartly from Causeland with the 2.52pm from Liskeard to Looe on 19 April 1960. Causeland was the only intermediate station when passengers were first carried on this line between Moorswater and Looe in 1879. This was long before the connection was made to the main line.

Although both Liskeard and Looe are easily accessible by road, it is to these little intermediate stations that we owe the present existence of this branch line, since Coombe Junction, St Keyne and Causeland are all situated on narrow Cornish country lanes. These were quite unsuited to the public transport vehicles of the 1960s, which would have presented problems when it came to providing a replacement bus service, if the branch had been closed.

Wall's
ICE CREAM
GUINNESS
BY-THE-SEA
The ideal holiday resort
TRELAWNE
HOLIDAY
ESTATE

Left:
On a rather hazy morning, 2 September 1961, 2-6-2T No 4574 draws the 10.45am departure into the single line platform at Looe. This view is taken looking down the estuary towards the mouth of the river, with railway sidings then occupying the area between the road and the river bank all the way down to the road bridge between East and West Looe. The daily goods train had, by 1961, been reduced to three days a week, but urgent fish traffic, carried in four wheeled vans, was attached to the passenger trains when required.

Outside the station the BR delivery and collection lorry is having a rest day, as the forecourt is taken over by other vehicles, carrying homeward-bound holiday-makers to the station on changeover day.

Doubtless, No 4574 will benefit from a draught of 'Guinness' from the water tank, before setting off up the valley to Coombe Junction and Liskeard.

Above:
All passenger trains between Liskeard and Looe have to reverse at Coombe Junction and, in steam days, this was often achieved swiftly and noisily as the '45xx' class tank engines ran around the coaches standing in the platform. No 4559 demonstrates this acceleration as she tackles the climb up to Liskeard with the 12.40pm from Looe on 7 May 1960.

Left:
The crew of No 4565, which had just run down from Moorswater, engage in conversation with the Coombe Junction signalman while awaiting the 'right away' for Liskeard at 1.5pm on 7 May 1960.

In the background the run-round loop, platform and waiting shelter of Coombe Junction Halt can be seen. The line stretching away into the distance under Moorswater viaduct, which carries the main line west of Liskeard, leads to Moorswater shed and the clay dry across the valley.

Right:
Moorswater was quite the most picturesque locomotive depot in Cornwall and, although its location looks delightfully secluded, the A38 trunk road ran through the trees beyond. Originally built in about 1861 to serve as the locomotive and carriage workshops for the Liskeard & Looe and Liskeard & Caradon railways, which made an end-on junction here, the shed was retained when the GWR took over the working of both lines in 1909.

2-6-2T No 5557 is working the thrice weekly goods on 15 March 1960 but, at this moment, the train crew is having lunch in the guard's van, which is almost hiding the other picturesque feature of Moorswater shed — a feature illustrated below.

Below:
This is the 'Loo' on the East Looe river — the firebox wrapper from 0-6-0T *Caradon*, the Liskeard & Caradon Railway's first new locomotive, strategically placed over the swift flowing stream. It must have been a mite draughty sitting there in winter!

5557

L.& S.W.R.
BEWARE OF
TRAINS
CROSSING
NO GATES

Left:
If one follows the trackbed of the extinct Liskeard & Caradon Railway up to Cheesewring Quarry, on the edge of Bodmin Moor, the eastern skyline is dominated, some six miles distant, by Kit Hill. This is another mining area of great antiquity, where mining, which reached its zenith in the mid-19th century, gave rise to the construction of the East Cornwall Mineral Railway, opened in 1872, with a gauge of 3ft 6in, from Kelly Bray, at the foot of Kit Hill, to Calstock Quay, reached by means of an incline down to the River Tamar.

Although the Plymouth, Devonport & South Western Junction Railway, which had powers to take over the ECMR, completed its main line from Lydford to Devonport in 1890, it was not until 1900 that a Light Railway Order was obtained to enable conversion of the ECMR to a standard gauge passenger carrying line. This was eventually opened in 1908 and, although the PD&SWJR's main line was worked by the London & South Western Railway, the company worked the branch itself with 0-6-0T *A. S. Harris* and 0-6-2Ts *Lord St Levan* and *Earl Of Mount Edgcumbe*.

The LSWR's 'O2' class 0-4-4Ts became the regular passenger engines on the line from 1929, and remained so, assisted by the 0-6-2Ts, until relieved by the Ivatt 2-6-2Ts.

Against a patchwork of fields in the Tamar Valley, 'O2' class 0-4-4T No 30225 is running into Latchley station with the 4.23pm from Callington (Kelly Bray) on 15 April 1961. Although the crossing is ungated, drivers of road vehicles cannot say they have not been warned, with three roadside signs in advance of the crossing.

Above:
The same train is seen again below Gunnislake, the principal station on the line and the only crossing place for passenger trains. We are now looking across the Tamar towards Dartmoor, with the then derelict, but now restored, river port of Morwellham nestling on a bend in the river hidden by the train.

Above:
Until the building of Calstock viaduct, most of the commercial traffic into and out of Calstock had come up the river. The arrival of the railway killed much of the river traffic, but the Tamar Market Boat survived until World War 2, operated by the paddle steamer *Whitsand Castle*, which had previously operated the Kingsbridge-Salcombe ferry for the GWR as the *Kenwith Castle*. It was, therefore, a very peaceful scene on 15 April 1961 as 'O2' class 0-4-4T No 30225 crossed the Tamar with the 4.23pm from Callington.

Right:
The Cornish border town of Launceston had already been the terminus of a broad gauge line from Plymouth for 21 years before the LSWR-sponsored North Cornwall Railway arrived in 1886. Subsequently, the two stations lay side-by-side but were unconnected until 1943.

In June 1952 the ex-GWR station was closed to passengers and thereafter all passenger trains used the ex-SR station.

On 18 June 1958 'Battle of Britain' class Pacific No 34061 *73 Squadron* does not appear to be overtaxed working the 4.24pm from Okehampton to Wadebridge, while 2-6-2T No 4591 is standing at the head of a similar two coach load on the 5.40pm to Plymouth. The ex-GWR locomotive shed (seen beyond the signalbox) remained in use until December 1962. *Trevor B. Owen*

34061
2
5
NORWICH
UNION

Above:
Typical of the stations between Launceston and Wadebridge, Otterham changed very little over the years and still has the air of a LSWR station even as 'Battle of Britain' class 4-6-2 No 34078 *222 Squadron* rolls in with the 3.32pm from Okehampton on 25 July 1964. *Trevor B. Owen*

Above right:
It was quite fitting that three of the '1366 class' 0-6-0PTs should come to Wadebridge to take over from the Beattie well tanks, since the '1366' class was directly descended, via the '1361' class 0-6-0STs of 1910, from the 0-6-0Ts purchased in 1873 from Sharp Stewart & Co by the Cornwall Minerals Railway. There was, moreover, a proposal in 1873 to link the CMR with the Bodmin-Wadebridge line, via the latter's Ruthern Bridge branch, but, like many such schemes, it did not proceed.

On 19 September 1964, 0-6-0PT No 1369 is about to haul the Plymouth Railway Circle's brake van special to Wenford Bridge, celebrating '130 Years of Steam'.

No 1369 is now preserved on the South Devon Railway at Buckfastleigh.

Right below:
In the unmistakeable garb of a Locomotive Inspector, the late Sam Smith makes for the signalbox as ex-LSWR 'T9' class 4-4-0 No 30719 assembles the stock in Padstow yard for the 3.13 pm departure, which the locomotive will haul through to Exeter Central on Friday 15 July 1960. Meanwhile, an ex-LSWR coach body, long since deprived of its underframe, still serves the railway at ground level. *R. C. Riley*

1368
WENFORD
SPECIAL
130 YEARS of STEAM
1369
PLYMOUTH RAILWAY
CIRCLE

30719
30719

Left:
Before the arrival of the railbus in this area, the traditional passenger service along the route of the Bodmin & Wadebridge Railway had been for the stopping service to be provided by the Southern trains running between Bodmin North and Wadebridge/Padstow, while some of the Western trains between Bodmin Road and Wadebridge ran non-stop between Bodmin General and Wadebridge. Ex-GWR 2-6-2T No 4569 is speeding through Nanstallon Halt with one of these non-stop services, the 2.30pm from Bodmin Road, on 10 September 1960. The train comprises a single 'B' set still in the red livery which preceded the later maroon style.

Above:
Normally the Wadebridge-Bodmin North passenger trains were powered either by an 'O2' class 0-4-4T or more often in later years by one of Wadebridge's two ex-GWR '8750' class 0-6-0PTs. An 'N' class 2-6-0 looks distinctly out of place working the 9.50am from Wadebridge to Bodmin North past Dunmere Junction in weather that tells us it must be St Swithin's Day, 15 July 1963. The line beyond this exceptionally clean 'Mogul' is the commencement of the Wenford Bridge line. *Trevor B. Owen*

Above:
After leaving the 'main line' to Bodmin North at Dunmere Junction, the Wenford Bridge line passed through a gate and then swung round into this cutting. The daily goods normally waited here for 20min or so, before plucking up enough courage to stop the traffic on this busy main road and, guarded by a flagman on either side, crossing slowly into the wooded seclusion of this delightfully rural line.

The locomotive in charge of this train is Beattie 2-4-0WT No 30585, one of three engines of this 75-strong class which worked this line from 1895 to 1962. The transfer to Cornwall came after completing 20 years of service on LSWR suburban trains in the London area, the work for which they were built in 1874. Remarkably, apart from these three engines, every other member of the class had been withdrawn from service before the turn of the century.

Right:
Later the same morning, 13 July 1961, eagerly awaited by the 'Railway Children' of Hellandbridge, No 30585 puffs gently away from the site of Helland Siding, after delivering a large parcel to the lady waiting to receive it, before squeezing past the cottages and across this very minor road. Proceeding slowly on its way up to Wenford Bridge terminus, it will pick up a few vans on the way, and propel them up to the end of the line.

30585

30200

Left:
For a town of its size, Bodmin was remarkably well served with stations and trains. This is the Southern station in the town, which acquired the suffix 'North' after Nationalisation, and which, in 1960, still had five trains a day to Wadebridge. Two of these went on to Padstow, with another on Saturdays. This is the 2pm departure to Padstow with ex-LSWR 'O2' class 0-4-4T No 30200 in charge on 10 September 1960. Although the 'O2' class had been the regular power on these trains for many years, by September 1960 they had been replaced by ex-GWR 0-6-0PTs Nos 4666 and 4694. Possibly Wadebridge has brought No 30200 out of store while one of the panniers was under repair.

Above:
In the wooded valley of the River Camel the Bodmin & Wadebridge Railway trains had been trundling between these towns since 1834 — the first steam hauled trains in Cornwall. More than 50 years were to elapse before the advance of the LSWR towards North Cornwall roused the GWR into building their own branch from Bodmin Road to a separate station on higher ground to the south of Bodmin. This was opened in 1887 and, a year later, the connecting line down to Boscarne Junction was completed. It is on this line that 2-6-2T No 4569 is climbing vigorously out of the valley with the 1.23pm from Wadebridge to Bodmin Road on 10 September 1960.

W 6881 W

Left:
This is the approach to Bodmin General station, previously the GWR station at Bodmin, with 2-6-2T No 4565 arriving with the 11.35am from Padstow earlier on Saturday 10 September 1960. There were normally two 2-6-2Ts and two 'B' (branch) sets working on this line, and both feature in this picture. No 4569 (which is now stowed on the siding alongside the engine shed) had arrived on the 12 noon from Bodmin Road to Bodmin. Normally, since Bodmin was a terminal station, it was necessary for the train engine to run round its train but, on this working, the trains will exchange engines and No 4569 will be leaving for Bodmin Road, whence it will return at 12.38pm with a service to Wadebridge. Meanwhile, No 4565 will run round the other 'B' set, before stowing it again in the siding, to allow the 12.38pm to pass, afterwards taking a short working to Bodmin Road and back, before picking up a guard's van and proceeding to Boscarne Junction.

Above:
On 27 May 1961, during a temporary lull in the passenger service at Bodmin as No 4565 is away down to Wadebridge, the other engine, this time No 4552, is in the middle of a complex shunting operation. This involves bringing two sets of eight loaded clay wagons up from Boscarne junction, adding to them a van from Bodmin yard and then taking the whole train down to Bodmin Road.

At this point No 4552 is about to fly shunt the van on to the guard's van standing on the run-round loop. Note the member of staff working on the bracket signal, where he is well positioned to enjoy the profusion of rhododendron bushes that cover both sides of the cutting.

BODMIN
P205578

Left:
I make no apology for including a third picture of Bodmin General because it was the most picturesque of the Cornish branch line termini, although not actually at the end of a line. Sadly, it lost much of its charm when the signalbox, engine and goods sheds were all needlessly destroyed, prior to the present preservation society coming upon the scene. The destruction of the engine shed was particularly shameful, since it was only vacated by the Great Western Society — which kept 0-6-0ST No 1363 and Devonport Dockyard 0-4-0ST No 19 there for many years — because the rent was suddenly raised to a figure the society could not afford. Predictably, no alternative tenant could be found so the building was demolished.

The whole of the layout of Bodmin GWR was very compact and, consequently, very suitable for modelling. The unusual signalbox nameboard is a point to note, and the ribbed extension of the platform down to ground level. The south end of the goods shed appears on the right of this picture, which was also taken on 10 September 1960. What lurks, I wonder, beneath the tarpaulin on wagon E203090, and what has the signalman found so interesting behind the lamp hut?

Above:
It is 8.55am at Bodmin Road on 4 July 1959 and 4-6-0 No 4950 *Patshull Hall* awaits the 'right away' on the Friday night 11.50pm from Paddington to Penzance, via Bristol, which conveyed sleeping cars to Plymouth. Not exactly a fast service, it had lengthy stops to exchange mail and parcels; even the public timetable showed 84min of station time in its schedule before leaving Plymouth and, from Saltash to Penzance, it stopped at every station.

The origins of today's Parkway status can be seen in the long since demolished goods shed and sidings which are now the car park.

At Lostwithiel station on 18 March 1961, the 'Bay' signal is off as 0-4-2T No 1468 prepares to leave on the 12.25pm for Fowey with auto-trailer No W163W — the hammered glass top-lights show up well on this 1929-built vehicle — while beyond, 2-6-2T No 5570 stands with an unmistakable rake of empty clay wagons.

The Cornish daffodils seem to be standing up well to the replacement of gas pipes by electric cables beneath their roots, while a '3 Car' sign shows the DMUs have arrived. On the up side of the main line, beyond the black goods shed, the buildings of the old Cornwall Railway carriage works can be seen.

The 9.30am from Paddington to Falmouth and Newquay was not introduced into the postwar timetables until the summer of 1953. It filled a long gap in the service to Cornwall between the 5.30am to Penzance and the 10.30am 'Cornish Riviera Express' which, by 1959, arrived in Penzance only 30min behind the 5.30am!

On 6 August 1959, having slowed for the 45mph restriction through Lostwithiel, 4-6-0 No 7813 *Freshford Manor* is accelerating hard on the climb up to Treverrin tunnel. It was unusual, in my experience, to find a 'Manor' alone on an express duty. Possibly it was substituting for a failed diesel — Whatever the reason, my notebook comment at the time was, 'Being Flogged'. In those days the Fowey branch track, dropping away on the right, was completely separate from the main line and sometimes a westbound train starting away from Lostwithiel would be raced out to the parting of the ways by the branch auto to Fowey. A fine stand of telegraph poles will be noted accompanying the main line.

Left:
Seen from high on the hills separating Lostwithiel from Par, an unidentified 'County' class 4-6-0 is climbing to Treverrin tunnel with the Saturdays only 12.5pm stopping passenger service from Plymouth North Road to Redruth on 2 August 1958. In practice, this train had a rather longer journey than that indicated in the public timetable, since it started from Launceston at 10.15am, stopping for eight minutes at Marsh Mills where it shed its branch engine for something more suitable for the main line. Though, on at least two occasions, it was worked forward by one of the St Blazey '42xx' class 2-8-0Ts. Probably this was a convenient return working on a Saturday after delivering empty clay wagons to Tavistock Junction yard. Behind the electricity pylon can be seen the then recently-closed Treverrin signal-box, while to its left a line of trees grows along the trackbed of the original broad gauge Cornwall Railway single line before it curved left across Milltown viaduct.

Above:
On 8 August 1959 2-6-2T No 5572 propels the 4.35pm auto working from Fowey into Lostwithiel, leaving the river bank to climb the short gradient up into the station.

No 5572 was one of 15 members of the '4575' class to be fitted with auto gear for working the Regular Interval Services on the Cardiff Valleys lines in 1953. When these services were dieselised in 1958, the steam engines were dispersed and No 5572 was on loan to St Blazey from Laira in August 1959. This locomotive is now part of the Great Western Society's collection at Didcot.

Above left:
Collett 0-4-2T No 1419 was the regular Lostwithiel-Fowey branch engine for most of the 1950s and, after arriving in Fowey station on 15 September 1958, has pulled forward and then dropped back into the bay platform. This is probably to allow through passage for a clay train from the jetties beyond the station, going to St Blazey. *Trevor B. Owen*

Below left:
The line into Fowey from the St Blazey direction was built by the Cornwall Minerals Railway, which initially ran a through service from Newquay to Fowey. Under the GWR, the workmen's passenger service to St Blazey finished in 1934, though the normal passenger service had ceased several years earlier, after which it became a goods-only line until converted to a private road by the clay company in 1968.

On 18 March 1961, 0-4-2T No 1468, temporarily transferred from Exeter to replace No 1419, is seen showing off her livery as the station porter is persuading two Indian seamen that they have reached their destination. Probably they were expecting a port the size of Liverpool, rather than the wooded estuary of the River Fowey, as the point where they would join their ship.

Above:
Principally for use on the heaviest clay loads over the steeply graded line between St Blazey and Fowey, there were only two 2-8-0Ts west of Bristol and both were allocated to St Blazey shed. On 8 July 1955 2-8-0T No 4247 is controlling a load of empties down from Pinnock tunnel, the longest in Cornwall, towards Par Sands. Since the gradient was against the loaded trains through the tunnel, these were normally worked bunker first towards Fowey, in order to avoid causing the engine crews unnecessary breathing problems.

After many years in the Barry scrapyard of Woodham Bros, No 4247 is currently under restoration on the Cholsey & Wallingford Railway. *R. C. Riley*

In the spring of 1969, after appearing in steam at a St Blazey Open Day, the Port of Par shunter *Alfred* is coming slowly forward towards the little Par Harbour engine shed, which lay at right angles to the main line behind it. For many years the harbour lines had an extension under the main line to reach a line of clay dries on the far side and the restricted headroom under this bridge made the cut-down design necessary. *Alfred* and sister engine *Judy* were both built by W. G. Bagnall Ltd. Earlier there had been a *Punch*, but this locomotive was scrapped in 1944.

A Shell/BP lorry waits patiently as the Par Bridge signal man accepts the token from the fireman of 0-6-0PT No 1626 heading a Plymouth Railway Circle brakevan special from Fowey over the goods only line to St Blazey. This train was later to run along the Newquay branch and eventually also traversed the length of the Goonbarrow branch.

In the far background can be seen the coaling stage of St Blazey shed, which lay to the left of the running lines.

Above:
Beyond Par, which is almost at sea level, the main line starts to climb in earnest, mostly at gradients in the 1 in 60s, until reaching St Austell, the commercial centre for this part of the county. Leaving St Austell, the line still climbs, but not so steeply, crossing St Austell viaduct where we see 'Castle' class 4-6-0 No 5058 *Earl of Clancarty* crossing with the 11.30am from Paddington to Penzance on 6 August 1959. For a few months in the summer of 1937 No 5058 bore the name *Newport Castle*. This seems rather a short train, but it was booked to shed half its load (including the Dining Car) in Plymouth. This was a bit hard on travellers to the far west, who would still have had another four hours' journey in front of them when the Dining Car closed down upon leaving Newton Abbot at 3.10pm.

Right:
Immediately above the seventh arch of St Austell viaduct in the above picture can be seen the white post of the signal controlling exit from the Trenance (or Lansalson) branch. This line left the main line to head northwards into the clay country for a mere 1 mile 53 chains. The only clay branch to be built by the GWR, work commenced in 1913 but was interrupted by World War 1 and, consequently, the line did not open to traffic until 1920. It closed in 1968, but a redundant clay dry in this valley is now the Wheal Martyn China Clay museum and this is well worth a visit.

In this view the Plymouth Railway Circle 'Cornwall Mineral' special, which covered many of the clay lines on 28 April 1962, is being propelled to the end of the branch at Lansalson yard by 2-6-2Ts Nos 5531 and 4564. These engines had hauled the train as far as Bojea yard, where they ran round, and then propelled it the rest of the way. Note the old engine house on the hillside with its extended chimney and the conical sand hills of waste material then so typical of this area.

Above:
Two miles west of the Trenance valley another clay line from the north joins the main line adjacent to the site of Burngullow station. This station closed in 1931. Although built by the Newquay & Cornwall Junction Railway, this broad gauge line, opened in 1869, terminated at Drinnick Mill, when the company ran out of funds. The intended extension to St Dennis Junction was eventually completed by the Cornwall Minerals Railway in 1874 on the standard gauge, with a break of gauge at Drinnick Mill until 1892.

In 1907 the Carpella United Clay Co, after taking its case to the House of Lords, obtained permission to extract clay from land crossed by the railway, creating the 'Carpella Gap' until 1922 when the GWR opened a deviation around the pit.

It is at this point that we find large and small standard pannier tanks Nos 9755 and 1624 descending from Drinnick Mill with an afternoon loaded clay train on 13 July 1961. The train includes, at the front, three empty wagons which will be shunted into New Carpella siding.

The proximity of the pit to the route of the deviation can be seen on the left, while on the other side it appears some of the villagers may have lost their back gardens when it was built.

Right:
The same train, now with loaded clay wagons only, is on the weighbridge at Burngullow, in a view looking east towards St Austell. Modernisation of what had been four separate clay drying plants is already under way. The original Cornish Kaolin and Wheal Louisa were served by the siding curving around to the left, while Parkyn & Peters and Methrose were in the background. The Western National bus leaving the works on route 66A to Carslake is No 365, a 1942 Bristol L5G chassis with a lengthened 1955 Eastern Coachworks body. Today this scene is dominated by the huge ECC Blackpool plant, while the main line is reduced to a single track westwards from the point where the down refuge siding used to join it.

66A
1624

6824

Left:
The main line beyond Burngullow commences to descend towards the valley of the River Fal in a series of curves following the hillside contours, crossing a small tributary on Coombe St Stephens viaduct.

When based at Carmarthen MPD during the war, 4-6-0 No 6824 *Ashley Grange* had been a very rare visitor to Cornwall but, from the early 1950s until the end of steam in 1962, this engine was allocated to Penzance. It is seen crossing this viaduct on 8 July 1961 with the Saturday 10.15 Launceston-Redruth working.

Above:
Unusual weather conditions produced this late fall of snow on 3 March 1962, providing a scene at Grampound Road which is more reminiscent of the Settle & Carlisle line. The station at Grampound Road had once been an important centre for the agricultural industry between St Austell and Truro, with a large goods yard at the eastern end of the station. On this day, 4-6-0 No 6814 *Enborne Grange* is heading the 10.55am 'all stations' (except Dockyard Halt) service from Plymouth to Penzance. This train was due to be overtaken at Par by the overnight Manchester-Penzance service.

Left:
At 8pm on 13 July 1961 the late evening sun peeps under the clouds as 0-6-0PT No 7715 leaves Truro with the last train of the day for Chacewater and Newquay.

The Truro station layout dated from around 1900. It was in that year that the old locomotive depot adjacent to the station was closed, enabling the station to be extended with through goods lines and sidings on its northern side.

The distant plume of steam comes from 4-6-0 No 1006 *County of Cornwall* on an up fitted-van train from the west. The train had been brought in by No 1008 *County of Cardigan* — a Penzance engine replaced by a Laira one.

The coaches on the right are standing in the bay platform normally used by the Falmouth trains. No 7715 is using the down main line, while the adjacent track was for branch trains. The outer face of the island platform was then the up main line.

Above:
As the 8pm to Newquay pulls out past the starting signal for platform No 3, we can see the leading vehicle is from the London Midland Region, one of several working on the branch at that time. The through goods lines are those adjacent to Truro West signalbox, from which diverges the entry track to the new (in 1900) engine shed, suitably wreathed in smoke and steam.

Above and right:
On Saturday morning 28 April 1962, 4-6-0 No 6863 *Dolhywel Grange* comes storming out of Highertown tunnel — a 70yd bore through the hill beyond Truro shed — with the 10.18pm Friday parcels from Paddington to Penzance. With the main line signal 'off' for the track around to the right, and Penwithers Junction ahead, the driver of *Dolhywel Grange* has the whistle valve open to warn passengers on the Plymouth Railway Circle 'Cornwall Mineral' special of his approach. The special is standing on the Falmouth branch, after climbing up from Truro Newham goods depot on the track leading in from the left.

Although both the Cornwall Railway and the West Cornwall Railway companies were incorporated on the same day in August 1846, it was the shorter West Cornwall Railway from Penzance which completed its single-track standard gauge line first, to arrive outside Truro, establishing its temporary Truro Road, Highertown station in this vicinity in August 1852.

Three years later the WCR had completed its new Truro terminus at Newham, down by the river and WCR trains terminated there until May 1859, when the Cornwall Railway opened its broad gauge line to Truro and completed Highertown tunnel as the first stage of its extension to Falmouth. This enabled WCR trains to run into Truro station, where there was a break of gauge until 1867, by which time the mixed gauge track had been laid to Penzance.

Above:
Although the Cornwall Railway completed Highertown tunnel (the first section of the remainder of its main line to Falmouth) in 1859, work ceased thereafter until 1861.

With eight viaducts and two tunnels in its 11$^{3}/4$ miles, the line was not open until August 1863, when the residents of Falmouth had high hopes for the commercial future of the town. However, despite its magnificent anchorage, and the development of the docks and repairing shipyard, Falmouth has never quite achieved its potential as a port. This is mainly the result of its lengthy communications to inland destinations. It, therefore, owes much to the GWR which promoted Falmouth as a holiday resort on the Cornish Riviera.

Once possessed of an overall roof, the terminus then had arrival and departure sides. Today, only the arrival side remains in use.

On 15 May 1959 2-6-2T No 5533 shunts the stock off the 5.46 arrival from Truro. To the left of the station a line extended down to the dockyard, one of the cranes in which can be seen towering above the station.
Michael Mensing.

Right:
A busy scene at Falmouth Docks on 4 June 1963, when the railway tracks around the yard were well used. Seemingly diminutive against the vast bulk of the *British Guardsman*, the Falmouth Dock & Engineering Co's 0-4-0ST No 4, built by Hawthorn Leslie in 1927, follows the shunter, who has his pole in hand.

BRITISH GUARDSMAN

5537

Left:
After closure of the Truro Newham terminus to passengers in 1863, it continued in use as a goods depot for over 100 years, finally closing in 1965. On 11 July 1961, Truro-based 2-6-2T No 5537 stirs the leaves with the return working of the mid-morning goods train, climbing away from the river, with Truro Cathedral dominating the distant skyline. Closure must be getting near, as the track has recently been relaid — a sure sign!

Above:
With Penwithers Junction signalbox just visible through the telegraph wires, and the original West Cornwall Railway alignment snaking into the trees on the left, 4-6-0 No 6938 *Corndean Hall* climbs along one of the rare straight sections in Cornwall with the 3.40pm from Plymouth to Penzance on 13 July 1961. The embankment on the right, carrying the Falmouth branch, was constructed in 1926 to replace the original Brunel-designed Penwithers viaduct.

For several years Truro's pride and joy, 4-6-0 No *1023 County of Oxford* was nearing the end of her days there on 29 August 1959. She is working the 4pm Truro-Penzance stopper, prior to being turned at Long Rock and taking up the night sleeper service through the Duchy. This turn was one of her regular duties. In the background is Chacewater station, junction for the Newquay line via Perranporth, with the separate branch track on the left.

Between Chacewater and Gwinear Road we have passed through the industrial heartland of Cornwall, a landscape scarred by centuries of mineral working, and still dotted with ruined engine houses, only some of which produced the wealth their owners expected of them.

At Gwinear Road 4-6-0 No 6814 *Enborne Grange* is restarting the 10.55am from Plymouth — last seen at Grampound Road — and here the overnight snow has almost gone; only in the shadow of the embankment is there a covering of the track in the Helston branch platform.

Above:
Constructed by the Helston Railway Co and opened in May 1887, though always worked by the GWR, the Helston branch developed a very considerable goods and passenger traffic. Evidence of the volume of goods handled can be gathered from this view of Helston station and yard taken on the afternoon of 24 July 1957, when three of the '45xx' class 2-6-2Ts were in use on the branch. No 4563 had brought in the 2.25pm from Gwinear Road and gone on to the shed; No 4545 was on an up goods working at Nancegollan, the crossing station, where most of the seasonal flower, potato and broccoli traffic was handled; whilst at Helston veteran No 4505 — one of the original Wolverhampton-built locomotives of 1907 — was shunting before taking out the 3.20pm passenger train.

Above:
Ex-GWR 0-6-0PT No 3635 lifts the wagons bound for Hayle Wharves out of the station goods yard on 14 July 1961, prior to backing the train down the steep 1 in 30 incline to the Wharf signalbox. This box controlled the main A30 road crossing at the foot of the bank. The incline can be seen curving down to the left, above the engine.

The original Hayle Railway line commenced from Wharf level and gained the higher ground towards Camborne by means of an incline. When the West Cornwall Railway built the present alignment, the incline was eliminated and the main line to Penzance was carried through Hayle on a viaduct, giving rise to the need for this steep connecting line to the wharves below.

Above:
As befits a picture taken at the end of the line, this view of Penzance station was taken almost at the end of the steam era on 14 July 1962. 4-6-0 No 1001 *County of Bucks* was among the last few steam engines allocated to Penzance MPD, and is standing at the head of the Saturday relief 4.45pm to Manchester.

The six-car cross-country DMU set is working the 4.20pm service to Plymouth, while a diesel shunter is attending the sheds built for handling local produce including that from the Isles of Scilly.

It had not been until 1937, when considerable land reclamation work and the building of a new sea wall were undertaken, that the GWR was able, at long last, to provide Penzance with a station suitable to receive the 'Cornish Riviera Express' and other long-distance trains. Prior to this it had even been necessary to start some trains from St Erth, such was the congestion at Penzance.

Right:
A typical morning line-up of 4-6-0s at Long Rock shed, Penzance, taken on 24 September 1960, with locomotives from four depots in the Newton Abbot Division.

Newton Abbot is represented by No 4920 *Dumbleton Hall*, which is now working on the Paignton & Dartmouth Railway after many years of effort by the Dumbleton Hall Preservation Society. No 4920 is flanked by 'Granges' from Penzance and Truro — respectively Nos 6824 *Ashley Grange* and 6828 *Trellech Grange* — while 'Modified Hall' No 6988 *Swithland Hall* had then only recently returned to Laira after a spell at Bristol (Bath Road).

The depot at Long Rock opened in 1914, replacing an earlier shed located just outside Penzance station. *R. C. Riley*

Above:
In 1877, when the railway first came to Lelant, the St Ives branch was broad gauge — the last branch line to be so constructed. There was also a quay at Lelant, the remains of which can be seen in the foreground, along which the broad gauge rails were also laid.

By 9 September 1961, although the original wooden station building was still standing, the siding had long gone, as 2-6-2Ts Nos 4566 and 4563 restart from Lelant with the 8.40am from St Erth to St Ives. The lamp code on the leading engine should have been changed at St Erth, since it is still showing the 'Empty Coaching Stock' code correct when leaving the Ponsandane sidings for St Erth, but incorrect once on the branch as a passenger train. However, this is not a normal branch train, but the stock for the 9.20am summer Saturdays through train to Paddington, making its way out to St Ives. On its return to St Erth at 9.35am, the main line engine(s) will be attached, together with a Restaurant Car and three more coaches to make up the full load for Paddington.

Right:
The sight every holidaymaker hopes to enjoy on arrival at destination — sun, sea and smooth golden sand — with steam evident from 2-6-2T No 4570 as she comes round the headland separating St Ives from Carbis Bay on 19 August 1961.

These visitors staying at Carbis Bay have returned from St Ives for 'high tea' on the 4.20pm hauled by 2-6-2T No 4571 on 30 July 1960. The platform building at Carbis Bay was only a waiting shelter; the station building and booking office were at the top of the path, halfway up which a porter is checking the passenger's tickets.

The normal winter 'B' set next to the engine has been supplemented with two non-corridor coaches for the summer season.

In the summer-time the intensity of the service on the St Ives branch often made the use of three engines essential, to avoid lost time in running around the train at either end. Ex-GWR 2-6-2T No 4570 waits in the bay, as No 4549 enters the long curving platform at St Ives with the 2.15pm from St. Erth — augmented by two Collett corridor coaches — on 4 August 1961. This was only weeks away from the official end of steam on the branch on 9 September. On that date the little ivy-clad engine shed serviced its final engine — No 4564.

Above:
From the moment the GWR took over the St Ives branch and purchased what was to become the Tregenna Castle Hotel, there was no doubt that their well-oiled publicity machine would extol the virtues of this area by every means possible.

The final accolade was the running of the 'Cornish Riviera Express' coaches as a through train from Paddington on summer Saturdays. After returning to StErth as the 5.50pm from St Ives, the 10-coach train has been stowed in one of the two down refuge sidings by 2-6-2Ts Nos 4549 and 4570. The buffer beam number on No 4549 is not a relic of GWR days, but was expertly painted by an enthusiastic fireman at Launceston, while the engine was allocated to Laira earlier in 1960.

Right:
On 12 July 1961 we see Laira-based 4-6-0 No 7916 *Mobberley Hall*, working the 5.45pm Penzance-Truro local train away from Gwinear Road station. In the background are the extensive sorting sidings, which lay around the curve to the east of the station and in which one of the Helston branch engines would often be shunting. Also visible are Gwinear Road East signalbox and the stationmaster's house.

7916

After leaving Truro in the early hours, 0-6-0PT No 3702 and brake van are now heading for home again on the up line through Camborne station on 15 July 1961. The train still has calls to make at Carn Brea yard and Drump Lane goods. Had it not been for the stiff westerly breeze blowing the steam down, the goods yard on the down side beyond the station, from which the pannier tank has just emerged, would be visible.

Camborne, as well as being at the centre of the copper and tin mining area of West Cornwall, was the birthplace of Richard Trevithick, inventor of the high-pressure steam locomotive, which he demonstrated in 1801.

This area of Cornwall was already well-served by the early railways, which provided transport for the mining industry to the north and south coasts, before the arrival of the main line from the east. Redruth was served by both the Hayle Railway (later taken over by the West Cornwall) and the four foot gauge Redruth & Chasewater Railway which provided access to Portreath and Devoran respectively.

Behind a display of flowers that would grace anyone's front garden, 2-6-2T No 5552 arrives in the branch platform at Chacewater with the 4.25pm through working from Truro to Newquay. The station porter is loading his barrow with items deposited from the 3.35pm stopper from Penzance, which was being hauled on this occasion by 4-6-0 No 6875 *Hindford Grange* and which had departed for Truro only a few minutes earlier.

This second route to Newquay — the first was the line from Par — was not completed by the GWR until January 1905, although it had been open as far as Perranporth since July 1903. At that time it diverged from the main line at a rather grand double-track triangular junction at Blackwater, about half a mile to the west, which gave direct access to Newquay from the Camborne/Redruth area.

However, this proved to be over-ambitious and the triangle, with its three signalboxes, had closed by 1924, in favour of an additional third line for the branch, laid alongside the main line into Chacewater station.

Ex-GWR 2-6-2T No 5552 is currently located at Bodmin General, undergoing restoration.

The Chacewater-Newquay line had an abundance of 'Pagoda' halts, six of which opened in August 1905. The first was at Mount Hawke, serving the village of the same name almost a mile away.

Even in 1961 goods traffic on the line was sufficient to support a daily working from Truro through to Newquay, returning after two hours, which allowed time for a trip out to St Columb Road, if required. Ex-GWR 0-6-0PT No 5744 is passing Mount Hawke with the return working at 3.20pm on 10 July 1961.

This engine was one of a pair of 0-6-0PTs transferred from Didcot to Truro in July 1960, both of which were fitted with spark arresting chimneys for working the MoD depot at Didcot. At first they worked from Truro with their bulbous chimneys, but the crews probably found that they would not steam very well with these attached and they were removed. Both engines continued to work with the chimney liner only until both were reallocated — No 3709 to Exeter, where she ran on the Exe Valley line still with no proper chimney, and No 5744 to Westbury.

Despite the single lamp on the top bracket, indicating a stopping passenger train, the driver of 0-6-0PT No 7715 still has the regulator open and is storming past Mithian Halt with the weekday 11am service from Newquay to Truro on 11 July 1961. This train only deigned to call at two of the seven Halts — Goonhavern and Perranporth Beach. The latter was opened in July 1931. The basic halt furniture at Mithian consisted of a 'Pagoda'-style hut, GWR notice, one or two oil lamps and the name-board — all of which are present, although the name-board has lost one of its substantial wooden posts and this seems to have been replaced by a length of 'two by two'.

Shepherds was the only crossing station on the Chacewater-Newquay line to have conventional side platforms. The main crossing station — at Perranporth — had an island platform, as did St Agnes after rebuilding in 1937.

This picture was taken from the train featured on page 65 entering Chacewater behind 2-6-2T No 5552. Passengers alighting here will have to cross the tracks, as there is no footbridge. This fact is evinced by the 'Beware of the Trains' sign at the platform end.

The Camp Coach, resplendent in fresh green paint, is No W9905W. Possibly the coach had not been serviced at Swindon as its companion, No W9906W, at Luxulyan was in chocolate and cream livery. Both were 1952 conversions from Dean turn-of-the-century corridor stock, replacing the prewar Camp Coaches. The coach is stationed in the erstwhile cattle dock. This feature was built mainly of Brunel bridge rail, as were the fence corner posts. Here, in contrast to Mithian Halt, the nameboard is supported by very substantial cast-iron posts.

When the Cornwall Mineral Railway built its line across Goss Moor to join the two separate sections of Treffry tramway into one railway, the proprietors could have had no idea of the volume of passenger traffic which would develop. By the late 1950s, up to 12 full-length trains were scheduled to leave Newquay between Friday evening and Saturday afternoon on peak weekends.

Hauled by 4-6-0s Nos 7816 *Frilsham Manor* and 6801 *Aylburton Grange* the 12.30pm (SO) from Newquay to Paddington is crossing the A30 road as it climbs towards Roche summit. *Trevor B. Owen*

On a glorious spring day, 28 April 1962, Bugle station yard was the lunch stop for the 'Cornwall Mineral' special, after traversing the line to Carbis Wharf. Some excellent Cornish pasties brought up from Redruth by Tom Opie were consumed before we resumed our journey back to St Dennis Junction.

This was the last steam working from St Blazey shed and, after the tour ended at Par, Nos 4564 and 5531 worked away to shed at dusk, with their four whistles echoing around the hills in a fitting finale.

In the far distance 0-6-0PT No 4673 steams away towards Bugle with the 2.40pm from Par to Newquay, while 0-6-0PT No 1664 resumes her homeward run with the Goonbarrow branch goods, after stopping for several minutes at Luxulyan to pass the other train and pin down brakes on 13 July 1961. Two members of the station staff are on duty, the signalman seen leaning from his box window and the porter outside the stone station building, almost hidden by the foreground cottages. The Camp Coach then stationed at Luxulyan is lost behind the steam from the engine.

It was a very warm afternoon on 8 August 1959 as 2-6-2T No 5500 came briskly up the Luxulyan valley under the Treffry viaduct with the 3.10pm from Par to Newquay. Before the Cornwall Mineral Railway constructed the line up through the Luxulyan valley in 1874, the Treffry tramway crossed it on this magnificent combined viaduct and aqueduct. The water was required to power the giant waterwheel, which raised and lowered the tramway wagons on the Carmears incline at Ponts Mill — at the foot of the valley — to the level of the tramway's upper section. The viaduct and tramway are still partly walkable and make a pleasant excursion on a fine afternoon.

The view from the Treffry viaduct is as spectacular as the viaduct itself, as, earlier that day, 0-6-0PT No 9755 descends the Luxulyan valley with the Saturdays-only 11.52am service from Newquay to Par. This train provided an 'all stations' service between the string of express trains leaving the resort on summer Saturdays. Some of the expresses also employed pannier tanks as assistant engines over the branch, with the main line engine leading. Two instances that day were 4-6-0 No 7022 *Hereford Castle* piloting 0-6-0PT No 9655 on the 12.40pm from Newquay to Cardiff, and 4-6-0 No 7816 *Frilsham Manor* piloting 0-6-0PT No 3635 with the 1.45pm from Newquay to Paddington.

Left:
The principal obstacle to be overcome by the holiday trains travelling eastwards out of Cornwall was the six-mile bank from below Bodmin Road to the summit at Doublebois station. Crossing Clinnick viaduct, well into the climb, are 4-6-0 No 6855 *Saighton Grange* and 2-6-0 No 6301 on the 9.20am from St Ives to Paddington on Saturday 8 August 1959.

Above:
Further up the Glynn Valley, on Saturday 13 September 1958, 4-6-0s Nos 7813 *Freshford Manor* and 6832 *Brockton Grange* stride across St Pinnock viaduct, the tallest on the main line, with the 10am from Newquay to Paddington. This train was normally a 15-coach load. *Trevor B. Owen*

Top Left:
Once over the summit at Doublebois it is mainly downhill to Saltash, and this mixed rake of carmine/cream and maroon stock, forming the 10am Newquay-Paddington service, is rolling merrily across Moorswater viaduct behind 4-6-0s Nos 7820 *Dinmore Manor* and 4928 *Gatacre Hall* on 15 August 1959. The overall speed limit in Cornwall at that time was 60mph, but there was a 50mph limit in force over the viaduct. Ahead of the engines, down in the valley, can be seen the old Moorswater clay dry, since replaced by modern plant.

Bottom Left:
Earlier that same Saturday morning another up train from Newquay presented the unusual sight of two 'first of class' engines double-heading together. The duo, 4-6-0 No 6800 *Arlington Grange* and 2-6-0 No 6300, are seen arriving at Liskeard with the 8.5am from Newquay to Newcastle.

The up platform at Liskeard was then very short and it will only be possible to get about half this 13-coach train into the platform. So, although the four minute allowance for station work seems generous, it will probably be extended if a second draw-up is required to load cycles or luggage into the rear van.

Above:
There was nothing strange about Wearde signalbox, since the name arose from Wearde Quay below, down on the River Lynher, alongside which the original Cornwall Railway single line ran to St Germans. The first part of this line, which diverged from the new 1908 main line immediately beyond the signalbox, was then still in use as sidings for excursion trains starting from Saltash. The down goods loop ending here extended back to Coombe-by-Saltash, past the site of Defiance platform, which had closed in 1930. Ex-GWR 4-6-0 No 4976 *Warfield Hall* is slowing on the approach to Saltash with the 7.50am from Newquay to Manchester on Saturday 25 July 1959.

I.K. BRUNEL
ENGINEER

Left:
I cannot pass Saltash without devoting some space to the auto-trains, which were such an integral part of Saltash life until the new road bridge suddenly made them redundant. On 29 September 1959 it is 0-6-0PT No 6400, enclosed by pairs of the postwar auto-coaches forming the 4.10pm departure to Plymouth, which will take these schoolchildren home to tea on the St Budeaux side. In those days the bus services to East Cornwall terminated near Saltash station, so that passengers could either transfer to the train or walk down to the river and take the chain ferry across the river and the bus into Plymouth.

On the down platform the station nameboard is rather lost in a sea of advertisements including 'Party Outings by Rail' and under the canopy is Cuneo's poster of the bridge, painted to celebrate its centenary that year.

Above right:
A picture which, I hope, captures the steam-heated warmth of an auto-saloon standing in Saltash station on a cold and wet November afternoon in 1959. The car is one of those built by the GWR in the 1929-33 period and, fortunately, the double sliding doors to the driver's vestibule are open, enabling us to see the regulator lever (hanging down), hand and vacuum brake controls. The interior panels were grained and varnished wood, and contrast with the black and white photographs which were a feature of every GWR coach interior.

Below right:
Finally, we end as we began, on the banks of the River Tamar, across which strides Brunel's masterpiece, the Royal Albert Bridge (floodlit in 1959 to celebrate its centenary), then alone and dominating the river, as it had done for the past 100 years.

I do hope that you have enjoyed your tour of Cornwall with me. *Colour-Rail/Peter W. Gray*

Back cover:
Backed by the main line crossing the valley on Liskeard viaduct, 2-6-2T No 4565 climbs briskly up to Liskeard with the 8.40am Saturday service from Looe on 15 August 1959. Curiously this train was advertised to the public as non-stop, except, of course, to reverse at Coombe Junction.